Text © 2008 by Debby Ware
Photographs © 2008 by James Roderick
Illustrations © 2008 by The Taunton Press

This material was previously published in the
book *Scrumptious Toppers for Tots & Toddlers*
(ISBN: 978-1-56158-998-2)
First published in this format 2014

The Taunton Press
Inspiration for hands-on living®

The Taunton Press, Inc., 63 South Main Street
PO Box 5506, Newtown, CT 06470-5506

e-mail: tp@taunton.com

Interior Design: Deborah Kerner
Photographer: James Roderick

*Threads*® is a trademark of The Taunton Press, Inc.,
registered in the U.S. Patent and Trademark Office.

The following name/manufacturer appearing in
*Caps & Hats for Babies* is a trademark: Velcro®

Library of Congress Cataloging-in-Publication Data
Ware, Debby, 1952- author.
  Caps & hats for babies : 7 adorable hats to knit /
Debby Ware.
     pages cm
  Includes index.
  ISBN 978-1-62710-958-1
1.  Knitting--Patterns. 2.  Baby bonnets. 3.  Infants'
clothing.  I. Title. II. Title: Caps and hats for babies.
  TT825.W372844 2014
  746.43'2--dc23
                                    2014025345
Printed in the United States of America
10 9 8 7 6 5 4 3 2 1

# CONTENTS

# Newborn Beanie

Create this beanie in bright, bold colors or soft pastels. Easy-to-make French Knots add a touch of whimsy. This is the perfect hat for bringing your new sweetie home in style.

## Sizing

Newborn to 6 months (14-in. circumference)

## Yarn

DK Weight smooth yarn

The hat shown is made with S.R. Kertzer Super 10 Cotton: 100% mercerized cotton, 4.4 oz. (125 g)/250 yd. (228.6 m).

## Yardage

### Pastel Beanie

60 yd. Super 10 Cotton White
15 yd. Super 10 Cotton #3532 Soft Yellow
5 yd. Super 10 Cotton #3722 Celery
5 yd. Super 10 Cotton #3443 Cotton Candy
5 yd. Super 10 Cotton #3841 Caribbean

### Bright Beanie

60 yd. Super 10 Cotton #3553 Canary
15 yd. Super 10 Cotton #3997 Scarlet
5 yd. Super 10 Cotton #3764 Peppermint
5 yd. Super 10 Cotton #3062 Turquoise

## Materials

16-in. U.S. size 4 circular needle
Four U.S. size 4 double-pointed needles
Four stitch markers
Tapestry needle

### GAUGE

22 sts = 4 in.

## Directions

### HAT BASE

With circ needles and Soft Yellow/Scarlet, CO 72 sts. Place a st marker on right needle and, beginning Rnd 1, join CO sts together, making sure that sts do not become twisted on needle.

Note: Always keep unworked yarn on the WS of your work and sl sts pw.

**Rnd 1:** P.

Drop Soft Yellow/Scarlet and attach Caribbean/Turquoise.

Cut all yarn and attach White/Canary.
  K15 rnds.
Drop White/Canary and reattach Soft Yellow/
  Scarlet. K1 rnd. P1 rnd.
Rep Rnds 2–5. Substitute White/Canary for
  Soft Yellow/Scarlet. Cut Soft Yellow/Scarlet.
  With White/Canary, K1 rnd and divide work
  into 4 sections, placing a st marker after
  each 18th st.

## SWIRL CROWN

At every st marker in each rnd, make the
  following dec: Sl marker, sl 1 pw, K1, psso.
  Move sts to dpns when necessary. Continue
  until 3 sts remain. Drop White/Canary, attach
  Soft Yellow/Scarlet and work I-Cord (see
  p. 29) for 3 in. Pick up White/Canary and
  work 1 in. Cut all yarn, leaving a 6-in. tail.
  Thread a tapestry needle and pass it through
  the remaining sts on the knitting needle. Pass
  needle and tails through the center of the
  I-Cord into the WS of the crown and secure.

## FINISHING

Weave in all loose ends. Make French Knots
  (see p. 28) in Celery, Cotton Candy, and
  Caribbean or Scarlet, Peppermint, and
  Turquoise. Tie the I-Cord into a knot so that
  the White/Canary tip peeks out.

**Rnd 2:** With Caribbean/Turquoise, *K1, sl 1 st;
  rep from * to end of rnd.
**Rnd 3:** With Caribbean/Turquoise, *P1, sl 1 st;
  rep from * to end of rnd.
**Rnd 4:** Cut Caribbean/Turquoise and pick up
  Soft Yellow/Scarlet. K entire rnd.
**Rnd 5:** With Soft Yellow/Scarlet, P entire rnd.
Rep Rnds 2–5 three times. Substitute Celery/
  Canary for Caribbean/Turquoise in first
  repetition and Cotton Candy/Peppermint for
  Celery/Canary in second repetition.

# Hearts & Flowers Hat

Silk flowers make a wonderful addition to this ruffled confection. Make it for your sweet valentine to wear year-round!

## Sizing

6 to 14 months (16-in. circumference)

## Yarn

DK Weight smooth yarn

The hat shown is made with S.R. Kertzer Super 10 Cotton: 100% mercerized cotton, 4.4 oz. (125 g)/250 yd. (228.6 m).

## Yardage

5 yd. Super 10 Cotton #3443 Shell Pink
90 yd. Super 10 Cotton #3997 Scarlet
40 yd. Super 10 Cotton #3454 Bubblegum

## Materials

16-in. U.S. size 4 circular needle

Four U.S. size 4 double-pointed needles

Stitch marker

Tapestry needle

Silk flower (found at any craft store)

Small piece of Velcro® (optional)

### GAUGE

22 sts = 4 in.

## Directions

### HAT BASE

With circ needles and Scarlet, CO 140 sts. Place a st marker on right needle and, beginning Rnd 1, join CO sts together, making sure that sts do not become twisted on needle.

**Rnd 1:** P.

**Rnd 2:** K.

**Rnd 3:** P.

**Rnd 4:** Drop Scarlet, attach Bubblegum, and K entire rnd.

**Rnd 5:** P.

Rep Rnds 4 and 5, alternating Scarlet and Bubblegum in Rnd 4, until you have 4 ridges of Bubblegum. Cut Bubblegum and pick up Scarlet. K1 rnd.

**Next Rnd:** Turn needles and work in opposite direction for the rest of the project. This ensures that the hat ruffle ends up with the

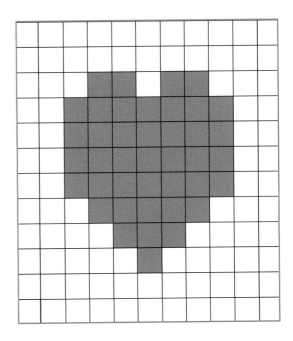

RS facing out. With Scarlet, K2tog entire
rnd—70 sts rem.

K until the hat measures 2 1/2 in. from the base
of hat where you first turned the needles
(approx 18–20 rnds). Place sts on dpns
when necessary.

## DECREASE ROUNDS

**Dec Rnd 1:** *K8, k2tog; rep from * for entire
rnd. K5 rnds.

**Dec Rnd 2:** *K7, k2tog; rep from * for entire
rnd. K5 rnds.

**Dec Rnd 3:** *K6, k2tog; rep from * for entire
rnd. K3 rnds.

**Dec Rnd 4:** *K5, k2tog; rep from * for entire
rnd. K2 rnds.

**Dec Rnd 5:** *K4, k2tog; rep from * for entire
rnd. K2 rnds.

**Dec Rnd 6:** *K3, k2tog; rep from * for entire
rnd. K1 rnd.

**Dec Rnd 7:** *K2, k2tog; rep from * for entire
rnd.

**Dec Rnd 8:** *K1, k2tog; rep from * for entire
rnd. K2tog until 4–6 sts rem.

Cut yarn, leaving a 6-in. tail. Using a tapestry
needle, thread the tail through the remaining
sts on the needles. Pull the yarn, gathering
sts tightly together, then secure the tail on
the WS of the hat.

## FINISHING

Weave in all ends. Following the graph
above and using Duplicate Stitch (see
p. 28), decorate the hat with hearts using
Bubblegum and Shell Pink. With Scarlet,
create French Knots (see p. 28) in the
"heart" of each heart.

Fold striped ruffle and secure to hat base at
regular intervals with a tapestry needle and
Scarlet. Attach a silk flower to the tip of the
hat using Velcro for easy removal, or sew
flower securely to tip of hat.

# Circles & Dots Beret

Chic baby couture is so easy to create. Simply add circles and red dots with a running stitch and French Knots. Très belle!

## Sizing

6 months (14-in. circumference) to
2 years (16- or 18-in. circumference)
Figures for larger sizes are given below in parentheses. Where only one set of figures appears, the directions apply to all sizes.

## Yarn

DK Weight smooth yarn
The hat shown is made with S.R. Kertzer Super 10 Cotton: 100% mercerized cotton, 4.4 oz. (125 g)/250 yd. (228.6 m).

## Yardage

80 (100, 100) yd. Super 10 Cotton #3873 Lapis
10 yd. Super 10 Cotton #3997 Scarlet
25 yd. Super 10 Cotton #3533 Daffodil

## Materials

16-in. U.S. size 4 circular needle
Four U.S. size 4 double-pointed needles
Stitch marker
Tapestry needle

### GAUGE

22 sts = 4 in.

## Directions

### HAT BASE

CO 70 (90, 110) sts with circ needle and Lapis. Place a st marker on right needle and, beginning Rnd 1, join CO sts together, making sure that sts do not become twisted on needle.

**Rnd 1:** P.
**Next Rnds:** K7 (10, 15) rnds.

### INCREASE ROUNDS

**Inc Rnd 1:** *K4, K1f&b; rep from * to end of rnd. You should have 84 (108, 132) sts. K2 rnds.

**Inc Rnd 2:** *K5, K1f&b; rep from * to end of rnd. You should have 98 (126, 154) sts. K2 rnds.

**Inc Rnd 3:** *K6, K1f&b; rep from * to end of rnd. You should have 112 (144,176) sts. K2 rnds.

Now you've completed a total of 17 (20, 25) rnds.

## RIDGE ROWS

Drop Lapis and attach Daffodil.

**Rnd 1:** K.

**Rnd 2:** P.

Cut Daffodil. Pick up Lapis and K1 rnd.

## TOP DECREASES

**Dec Rnd 1:** *K8 (6, 6), K2tog; repeat from * to end of rnd. K2 (4, 5) rnds.

**Dec Rnd 2:** *K7 (5, 5), K2tog; rep from * to end of rnd. K2 (4, 5) rnds.

Continue in established pattern, knitting one less st between decs and putting sts on dpns when necessary, until you have completed K1, K2tog, and approx 6 sts rem. Cut the yarn, leaving a 6-in. tail. Thread a tapestry needle and pass it through the remaining sts on the needle. Bring tail to the WS of the work and secure.

## FINISHING

Weave in all loose ends. Thread a tapestry needle with Daffodil and, using a running stitch, decorate the brim of the hat with circles.

Here's a tip: Use a quarter as a guide to make sure the circles are evenly spaced and roughly the same size.

Continuing with Daffodil, embroider a concentric circle on the top of the hat. Thread a tapestry needle with Scarlet and create French Knots (see p. 28) in the centers of the circles on the brim as well as the one in the center of the hat. Voilà!

# Heavenly Harlequin Hat

This hat is a little zany and a whole lot of fun. French Knots and squiggles on top guarantee that it will stand out in a crowd!

## Sizing

Newborn (12-in. circumference) to
2 years (14- or 16-in. circumference)
Figures for larger sizes are given below in
    parentheses. Where only one set of figures
    appears, the directions apply to all sizes.

## Yarn

DK Weight smooth yarn
The hat shown is made with S.R. Kertzer Super
    10 Cotton: 100% mercerized cotton, 4.4 oz.
    (125 g)/250 yd. (228.6 m).

## Yardage

40 (50, 60) yd. Super 10 Cotton #3936
    Wisteria
40 (50, 50) yd. Super 10 Cotton #3535 Key
    Lime
30 yd. Super 10 Cotton #3042 Nectarine
10 (20, 20) yd. Super 10 Cotton #3533
    Daffodil

## Materials

16-in. U.S. size 4 circular needle
Four U.S. size 4 straight needles
Stitch marker
Tapestry needle

### GAUGE

22 sts = 4 in.

## Directions

### HAT BASE

With circ needles and Key Lime, CO 70 (80,
    90) sts. Place a st marker on right needle
    and, beginning Rnd 1, join CO sts together,
    making sure that sts do not become twisted
    on needle.

**Rnd 1:** P.

**Rnd 2:** *Attach Daffodil and MB (see p. 28 for
    Bobble instructions). Drop Daffodil, pick up
    Key Lime, K4; rep from * to end of rnd.

**Rnd 3:** K with Key Lime.

**Rnd 4:** Drop Key Lime, pick up Daffodil.
    K entire rnd.

**Rnd 5:** P with Daffodil. Drop Daffodil, pick up
    Key Lime.

**Next 4 (5, 6) rnds:** K with Key Lime.

Now you've completed a total of 17
    (20, 25) rnds.

**Next Rnd:** Drop Key Lime, pick up Daffodil. K entire rnd.

**Next Rnd:** P with Daffodil.

Cut Daffodil and Key Lime. Attach Wisteria. K4 (6, 8) rnds.

## DECREASE ROUNDS

**Dec Rnd 1:** *K8, K2tog; rep from * to end of rnd. K4 rnds.

**Dec Rnd 2:** *K7, K2tog; rep from * to end of rnd. K4 rnds.

Continue in established pattern, knitting one less st between decs and changing to dpns when necessary until you have completed K3, K2tog. K2 rnds.

**Next Dec Rnd:** *K2, K2tog; rep from * to end of rnd. K2 rnds.

**Next Dec Rnd:** *K1, K2tog; rep from * to end of rnd.

**Next Dec Rnd:** K2tog for the entire rnd.

Cut yarn, leaving a 6-in. tail, and thread a tapestry needle. Pass the tapestry needle through the remaining sts. Bring to WS of work and secure.

## I-CORD

With Nectarine and 2 dpns, CO 3 sts. Make an I-Cord (see p. 29) approx 36 in. long. Thread a tapestry needle and pass it through the sts on the needle to BO. Cut the yarn, leaving a long tail to sew the I-Cord onto the hat. Decorate the hat with the I-Cord in a spiral pattern (see the photo on the facing page).

## SQUIGGLE TOPPERS

Make 3 Daffodil and 2 Key Lime I-Cords. Using 2 dpns, CO 2 sts and work until I-Cords are approximately 8 in. long. Cut yarn, leaving 4-in. tails. Thread each tail through a tapestry needle and slip through the sts on the needle to BO. Pass the needle through the I-Cords. Bring both tails through the peak of the hat, pulling tight to make each I-Cord scrunch up into a little squiggle.

## FINISHING

Weave in all loose ends. Thread a tapestry needle with Wisteria and, using Duplicate Stitch (see p. 28), make diagonal sts on the second Key Lime band. For the final touch, use Nectarine to make small French Knots (see p. 28) between the Daffodil bobbles on the bottom Key Lime band.

Ta-da! Heavenly Harlequin Hat!

# Lemon Drop Crown

This shimmering yellow beret is as warm and bright as the sun!
The sparkling details make it right for any special shindig.

## Sizing

3 to 18 months (14-in. circumference)

## Yarn

DK Weight smooth yarn

DK Weight eyelash yarn

The hat shown is made with S.R. Kertzer
Super 10 Cotton: 100% mercerized cotton,
4.4 oz. (125 g)/250 yd. (228.6 m) and
Stylecraft Icicle: 62% polyester, 38%
metallized polyester, 1.75 oz. (50 g)/87 yd.
(80 m).

## Yardage

70 yd. Super 10 Cotton #3533 Daffodil

40 yd. Super 10 Cotton #3532 Soft Yellow

20 yd. Icicle #1142 Sunlight

Small amount of Super 10 Cotton #3454
Bubblegum

## Materials

16-in. U.S. size 4 circular needle

Four U.S. size 4 double-pointed needles

Four stitch markers

Tapestry needle

Pom Pom maker (3 in.)

### GAUGE

22 sts = 4 in. with Super 10 Cotton

## Directions

### HAT BASE

With circ needle and Daffodil, CO 72 sts. Place
a st marker on right needle and, beginning
Rnd 1, join CO sts together, making sure sts
do not become twisted on needle.

Note: Always keep unworked yarn on the WS
of your work and sl sts pw.

**Rnd 1:** P.

**Rnd 2:** Drop Daffodil and attach Soft Yellow.
With Soft Yellow *K1, sl 1 wyib; rep from * to
end of rnd.

**Rnd 3:** With Soft Yellow *P1, sl 1 wyib; rep
from * to end of rnd.

**Rnd 4:** Drop Soft Yellow. K with Daffodil for the entire rnd.

**Rnd 5:** P with Daffodil.

**Rnds 6–13:** Rep Rnds 2–5.

Cut Daffodil and with Soft Yellow K1 rnd, placing a st marker after every 18th st to divide work into 4 equal parts.

Make the following inc at each marker: Work to 1 st before marker and K1f&b into next st, sl marker, K1, K1f&b into next st. Continue making inc at each marker until you have K8 rnds. You should have 136 sts.

Cut Soft Yellow and attach Icicle. K1 rnd. P1 rnd.

Cut Icicle and attach Daffodil. K8 rnds, keeping the markers on the needle.

CROWN DECREASES

**Dec Rnd 1:** *K up to 2 sts before each marker, sl 1, K1, psso, sl marker, K1, K2tog; rep from * to end of rnd. Continue in established pattern, changing to the dpns when necessary.

When 4–7 sts rem, cut the yarn, leaving a 6-in. tail. Using a tapestry needle, thread the tail through the remaining sts on the needles. Pull the yarn, gathering sts tightly together, then secure the tail on the WS of the crown.

FINISHING

With Daffodil and Icicle, make a Pom Pom (see p. 29). Attach it to the top of the crown. Using Icicle, place French Knots (see p. 28) along the Soft Yellow row, 3 on each side of the hat (see the photo on the facing page). With Icicle, make 1 French Knot on each quarter of the crown directly below the Pom Pom. With Bubblegum, place small French Knots below each Icicle French Knot (see the photo above).

# Swirls & Cherries Beret

This sweet beret is perfect for little girls, and is oh-so-quick to create!
Decorate the hat with swirls using an easy running stitch. The cherries
are the finishers that complete this delightful hat.

## Sizing

6 months to 2 years (16-in.
circumference)

## Yarn

DK Weight smooth yarn

The hat shown is made with S.R. Kertzer Super
10 Cotton: 100% mercerized cotton, 4.4 oz.
(125 g)/250 yd. (228.6 m).

## Yardage

60 yd. Super 10 Cotton #3443 Shell Pink

14 yd. Super 10 Cotton #3454 Bubblegum

30 yd. Super 10 Cotton #3997 Scarlet

3 yd. Super 10 Cotton #3722 Celery

## Materials

16-in. U.S. size 4 circular needle

Four U.S. size 4 double-pointed needles

One pair U.S. size 4 straight needles

Four stitch markers

Tapestry needle

### GAUGE

22 sts = 4 in.

## Directions

### HAT BASE

With circ needles and Scarlet, CO 80. Place
a st marker on right needle and, beginning
Rnd 1, join CO sts together, making sure
that sts do not become twisted on needle.

**Rnd 1:** P. Cut Scarlet and attach Shell Pink.

### STRIPE PATTERN

**Stripe 1:** Using Shell Pink, K1 rnd, P1 rnd.

**Stripe 2:** Drop Shell Pink and attach
Bubblegum. K1 rnd, P1 rnd.

Rep Stripes 1 and 2 for a total of 7 stripes,
ending with a Shell Pink stripe.

**Last Stripe:** Attach Scarlet and K1 rnd,
P1 rnd.

Cut Bubblegum and Scarlet. K1 rnd with Shell
Pink, dividing the work into 4 equal parts by
placing a st marker after every 20th stitch.

### INCREASE ROUNDS

**Next Rnd:** K to 1 st before marker, K1f&b, sl marker, K1, K1f&b into the next stitch. Continue working inc at each marker for 8 rnds. You should have 144 sts.

### RIDGE ROUNDS

Drop Shell Pink and attach Celery. K1 rnd, P1 rnd. Cut Celery. K1 rnd with Shell Pink.

### CROWN DECREASES

**Dec Rnds:** On each rnd and at every marker, make the following decs: Work to 2 sts before a marker, sl 1, K1, psso, sl marker, K1, K2tog.

Continue in established pattern, placing sts on dpns when necessary. When approx 5–7 sts rem, drop Shell Pink and attach Celery. Work I-Cord (see p. 29) for 12 rows. Cut all yarn, leaving a 6-in. tail. Thread a tapestry needle and pass it through the remaining sts. Carefully pass the needle and tails through the center of the I-Cord into the WS of the crown and secure. Weave in all loose ends.

### CHERRIES

With Scarlet and straight needles, CO 1 st. K1f&b twice, K1, into that st, creating 5 sts from 1. K5 rows (Garter st).

**Dec Rows:** Sl 1, K1, psso, K1, K2tog. Cut the yarn, leaving a 4-in. tail. Thread a tapestry needle and pass it through the sts. Tie the CO and BO tails together to form a ball. Make three cherries.

Attach each cherry to the tip of the Celery I-Cord by threading a tapestry needle and bringing the tail through the center of the I-Cord to the WS of the crown. Tie each cherry securely and scrunch the I-Cord a bit so that it looks like a stem.

### RUNNING STITCH SWIRLS

Thread a tapestry needle with Scarlet. Using the photo on the facing page as a reference, embroider as many swirls on the band as you like.

# Black & Bright Beret

Vibrant colors set against black make this hat absolutely smashing. Fun "fingers" are a great finishing touch.

## Sizing

6 months (14-in. circumference) to
2 years (16-in. circumference)
Figures for larger size are given below in
parentheses. Where only one set of figures
appears, the directions apply to both sizes.

## Yarn

DK Weight smooth yarn
The hat shown is made with S.R. Kertzer Super
10 Cotton: 100% mercerized cotton, 4.4 oz.
(125 g)/250 yd. (228.6 m) and S.R. Kertzer
Super 10 Cotton Multi: 100% mercerized
cotton, 3.5 oz. (100 g)/220 yd. (201 m).

## Yardage

40 (50) yd. Super 10 Cotton Black
30 yd. Super 10 Cotton #3873 Lapis
40 yd. Super 10 Cotton #3062 Turquoise
30 yd. Super 10 Cotton Multi #2016 Carousel

## Materials

16-in. U.S. size 4 circular needle
Four U.S. size 4 double-pointed needles
Four stitch markers
Tapestry needle

### GAUGE

22 sts = 4 in.

### SEED STITCH

*Rnd 1:* *K1, P1; rep from * to end of rnd.
*All other rnds:* K the P sts and P the K sts.

## Directions

### HAT BASE

With circ needle and Lapis, CO 72 (88) sts.
Place a st marker on right needle and,
beginning Rnd 1, join CO sts together,
making sure that sts do not become twisted
on needle.
Note: Always keep unworked yarn on the WS
of your work and sl sts pw.
**Rnd 1:** P. Drop Lapis and attach Turquoise.

**Rnd 2:** With Turquoise, *K1, sl 1; rep from * to end of rnd.

**Rnd 3:** With Turquoise, *P1, sl 1; rep from * to end of rnd.

**Rnd 4:** Drop Turquoise. K with Lapis.

**Rnd 5:** P with Lapis.

Rep Rnds 2–5 three times to create 3 Lapis ridges. Cut Lapis.

**Next Rnd:** K with Turquoise.

### RUFFLE

**Inc Rnd:** With Turquoise, *K2, K1f&b; rep from * to end of rnd. Work Seed st for 1½ (2) in. There should be 108 (132) sts on the needle.

Cut Turquoise. Attach Lapis and K1 rnd.

### FINGERS

Attach Multi. *Using the Cable Cast-On (see p. 28) and Multi, CO 5 sts, then BO 5 sts. K3 sts with Lapis. Rep from * for remainder of rnd. Cut Multi and K1 rnd with Lapis. BO all sts pw.

Holding the hat with the RS facing you, bend the Turquoise ruffle down and expose the hat base. With Black, pick up 72 (88) sts (Lapis loops) evenly spaced around the hat. K for approx 3 in.

### CROWN RIDGE

Cut Black and attach Lapis. K1 rnd, P1 rnd. Drop Lapis and attach Turquoise. K1 rnd. Cut Turquoise and pick up Lapis. K1 rnd, P1 rnd.

### MULTI CROWN

Cut all yarn and attach Multi. K1 rnd and divide work into 4 equal parts, placing a st marker after every 18 (22) sts.

### SWIRL TOP DECREASES

On every rnd, at every st marker, make the following dec (putting sts on dpns when necessary): Sl marker, sl 1, K1, psso. Continue until 4 sts rem. Cut Multi and attach Turquoise.

### TOP STEM

Place rem 4 sts onto a dpn. With Turquoise, work I-Cord (see p. 29) for 2 in. Cut all yarn, leaving a 6-in. tail. Thread tail through a tapestry needle and pass it through the

remaining sts on dpn needle. Carefully pass
needle and tails through the center of the
I-Cord into the WS of the crown and secure.

FINISHING

Weave in all loose ends. Push the Turquoise
ruffle down to bottom of hat and let the
fingers stand up straight and tall.

# Special Stitches

## Bobble

With desired color yarn, K1, P1, K1 in the next st to make 3 sts from 1. Turn and K3. Turn and K3, then lift the second and third sts over the first st on the right needle.

## Cable Cast-On

Insert right needle between first 2 sts on left needle. Wrap yarn as if to knit. Draw yarn through to complete st and slip this new st onto left needle.

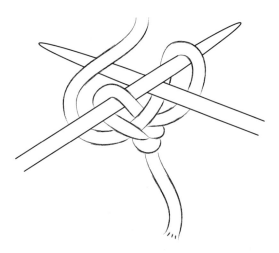

## Duplicate Stitch

Thread a tapestry needle with the desired color yarn. Bring the needle through from the WS of the work to the base of the knit st you wish to cover with a duplicate st on the front side. Insert

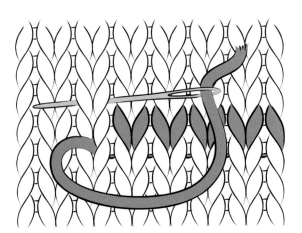

the needle directly under the base of the knit st that lies above the st you wish to cover. Bring the needle down and insert it at the base of the same knit st. Bring the tip of the needle out at the base of the next st you wish to cover and repeat this process until you have covered all the desired sts in the design.

## French Knot

Thread a tapestry needle with yarn and bring it from the WS of the work to the RS at the point where you wish to place the French Knot. Holding the yarn down with your left thumb, wind the yarn 3 times (for a small knot) or 4 to 6 times (for a large knot) around the needle. Still holding the yarn firmly, twist the needle back to the starting point and insert it close to where the yarn first emerged. Still holding the yarn down with your left thumb, slowly pull the yarn through to the WS to create a French Knot. Secure each knot on WS.

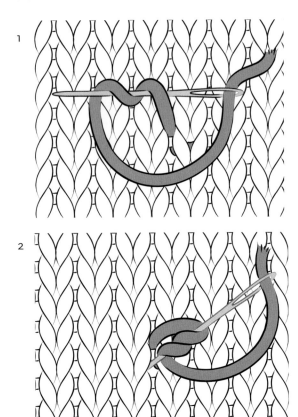

3

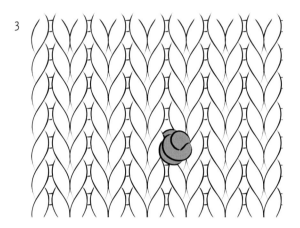

## I-Cord

With two dpns, work I-Cord as follows: K4 to 6 sts. *Do not turn work. Slide sts to other end of needle, pull the yarn around the back, and knit the sts as usual. Repeat from * for desired length of cord.

## How to Make Pom Poms

1.  Cut out two circles of cardboard (approx. 2½-in. diameter) and cut a ¾-in. circle out of the middle of each circle to make two rings.

2.  Hold both cardboard rings together and wrap the yarn of your choice around the two rings until the cardboard is covered. The more yarn you wrap, the fuller the pom pom will be.

3.  Carefully insert the blade of your scissors into the outer edge of the yarn-wrapped cardboard so that it sits between the two cardboard rings. Hold the center of the ring with your thumb and forefinger and carefully cut all the way around the outside edge.

4.  Once the wrapped yarn has been cut, slide a length of yarn between the cardboard rings and tie it around the center of the cut threads. Ease the cardboard rings off the yarn, and tie again to make a tight knot, leaving a long tail. Fluff the pom pom and trim any untidy ends.

# Abbreviations

| | | | |
|---|---|---|---|
| approx | approximately | MB | make bobble |
| beg | beginning | P | Purl |
| BO | bind off | psso | pass slipped stitch over |
| circ | circular | pw | purlwise |
| CO | cast on | rem | remaining |
| cont | continue | rep | repeat |
| dec | decrease/decreases/ decreasing | rnd | round |
| dpn(s) | double-pointed needle(s) | RS | right side |
| inc | increase/increases/ increasing | skp | slip 1, knit 1, pass slipped stitch over knit 1 |
| K | knit | sl 1 | slip 1 stitch |
| K1f&b | knit in the front and in the back of the same stitch | st(s) | stitch(es) |
| K2tog | knit 2 stitches together | St st | stockinette stitch |
| kw | knitwise | tog | together |
| M1 | make 1 stitch | WS | wrong side |
| | | wyib | with yarn in back of work |
| | | yd | yard/yards |
| | | YO | yarn over |

# Standard Yarn Weights

| NUMBERED BALL | DESCRIPTION | STS/4 IN. | NEEDLE SIZE |
|---|---|---|---|
| 1 SUPER FINE | Sock, baby, fingering | 27–32 | 2.25–3.25 mm (U.S. 1–3) |
| 2 FINE | Sport, baby | 23–26 | 3.25–3.75 mm (U.S. 3–5) |
| 3 LIGHT | DK, light worsted | 21–24 | 3.75–4.5 mm (U.S. 5–7) |
| 4 MEDIUM | Worsted, afghan, Aran | 16–20 | 4.5–5.5 mm (U.S. 7–9) |
| 5 BULKY | Chunky, craft, rug | 12–15 | 5.5–8.0 mm (U.S. 9–11) |
| 6 SUPER BULKY | Bulky, roving | 6–11 | 8 mm and larger (U.S. 11 and larger) |

**Look for these other *Threads* Selects booklets at www.tauntonstore.com and wherever crafts are sold.**

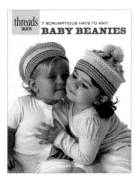

**Baby Beanies**
Debby Ware
EAN: 9781621137634
8½ x 10⅞, 32 pages
Product# 078001
$9.95 U.S., $9.95 Can.

**Cute Pets to Knit**
Susie Johns
EAN: 9781627107747
8½ x 10⅞, 32 pages
Product# 078043
$9.95 U.S., $9.95 Can.

**Pet Projects to Knit**
Sally Muir and Joanna Osborne
EAN: 9781627100991
8½ x 10⅞, 32 pages
Product# 078034
$9.95 U.S., $9.95 Can.

**Dog Coats & Collars**
Sally Muir and Joanna Osborne
EAN: 9781627100984
8½ x 10⅞, 32 pages
Product# 078033
$9.95 U.S., $9.95 Can.

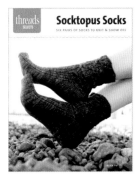

**Socktopus Socks**
Alice Yu
EAN: 9781627101004
8½ x 10⅞, 32 pages
Product# 078035
$9.95 U.S., $9.95 Can.

**Colorwork Socks**
Kathleen Taylor
EAN: 9781621137740
8½ x 10⅞, 32 pages
Product# 078011
$9.95 U.S., $9.95 Can.

**Fair Isle Flower Garden**
Kathleen Taylor
EAN: 9781621137702
8½ x 10⅞, 32 pages
Product# 078008
$9.95 U.S., $9.95 Can.

**Fair Isle Hats, Scarves, Mittens & Gloves**
Kathleen Taylor
EAN: 9781621137719
8½ x 10⅞, 32 pages
Product# 078009
$9.95 U.S., $9.95 Can.

**Felted Scarves, Hats & Mittens**
Kathleen Taylor
EAN: 9781627100960
8½ x 10⅞, 32 pages
Product # 078031
$9.95 U.S., $9.95 Can.

**Favorite Felted Gifts to Knit**
Kathleen Taylor
EAN: 9781627101653
8½ x 10⅞, 32 pages
Product# 078038
$9.95 U.S., $9.95 Can.

**Shawlettes**
Jean Moss
EAN: 9781621137726
8½ x 10⅞, 32 pages
Product# 078010
$9.95 U.S., $9.95 Can.

**Cable Shawlettes**
Jean Moss
EAN: 9781621137733
8½ x 10⅞, 32 pages
Product# 078037
$9.95 U.S., $9.95 Can.

**Look for these other *Threads* Selects booklets at www.tauntonstore.com and wherever crafts are sold.**

**Easy-to-Sew Flowers**
EAN: 9781621138259
8½ x 10⅞, 32 pages
Product# 078017
$9.95 U.S., $9.95 Can.

**Easy-to-Sew Gifts**
EAN: 9781621138310
8½ x 10⅞, 32 pages
Product# 078023
$9.95 U.S., $9.95 Can.

**Easy-to-Sew Handbags**
EAN: 9781621138242
8½ x 10⅞, 32 pages
Product# 078016
$9.95 U.S., $9.95 Can.

**Easy-to-Sew Kitchen**
EAN: 9781621138327
8½ x 10⅞, 32 pages
Product# 078024
$9.95 U.S., $9.95 Can.

**Easy-to-Sew Lace**
EAN: 9781621138228
8½ x 10⅞, 32 pages
Product# 078014
$9.95 U.S., $9.95 Can.

**Easy-to-Sew Lingerie**
EAN: 9781621138235
8½ x 10⅞, 32 pages
Product# 078015
$9.95 U.S., $9.95 Can.

**Easy-to-Sew Pet Projects**
EAN: 9781621138273
8½ x 10⅞, 32 pages
Product# 078018
$9.95 U.S., $9.95 Can.

**Easy-to-Sew Pillows**
EAN: 9781621138266
8½ x 10⅞, 32 pages
Product# 078019
$9.95 U.S., $9.95 Can.

**Easy-to-Sew Scarves & Belts**
EAN: 9781621138211
8½ x 10⅞, 32 pages
Product# 078013
$9.95 U.S., $9.95 Can.

**Easy-to-Sew Skirts**
EAN: 9781621138280
8½ x 10⅞, 32 pages
Product# 078020
$9.95 U.S., $9.95 Can.

**Easy-to-Sew Tote Bags**
EAN: 9781621138297
8½ x 10⅞, 32 pages
Product# 078021
$9.95 U.S., $9.95 Can.

**Easy-to-Sew Windows**
EAN: 9781621138303
8½ x 10⅞, 32 pages
Product# 078022
$9.95 U.S., $9.95 Can.